NEW FOUND LAND

Also by Carolyn Clark

Poetry

Mnemosyne: The Long Traverse (2013)

Amish Mimesis (2015)

Choose Lethe: Remember to Forget (forthcoming, 2017)

NEW FOUND LAND

Carolyn Clark

Cayuga Lake Books

Ithaca, New York

New Found Land
by Carolyn Clark

First Printing – August 2017
ISBN: 978-1-68111-195-7

Front Cover: slide photo by my father Mills Gardner Clark (RIP 2017); its bright, abstract impression due in part to film's exposure to the intense heat of a furnace in a Russian steel mill, 1957.

Back cover photo by Geoffrey Cullen

Printed in the U.S.A.

0   1   2   3   4

for this our little palm of Earth –
poems of resilience

Contents

New Found Land

(over Greenland, on a flight from Milan to NYC, 2014)

Following saffron dawn,
a silver winged vessel
over *New found land* :
ice whorls, white as boats, below,
icebergs scattered as never before,
seas that don't stop rising.

Next, ocean tundra,
fissures of olive hued rock
reaped by glacial harrowing,
labyrinth of fjords, dark blue,
surfacing as snowmelt unzips new land.

A little further, first sign of man:
a solitary dirt road
forking from point of ocean
toward a gleaming outpost–
aluminum and steel half cylinder
Quonset, long-bed storage unit,
today's covered wagon.

Nearby, more nestled specks–
    and a house called *home*.

Twig Poem

for Archie Ammons   *(Chamonix, 1978)*

Motions spring
    from melting snow:
        a twig regains
        consciousness,
    weight released
from former state.
Support comes
from the main stem
as the snow begins to loosen…
corn snow we call it back home.
It begins
to take on new form -
from hard buds
    whose melting
        makes way
    to motion.
Each day another
layer of destruction
revealed: littered needles,
lichen, moss and the like
cling to that thirsty rock,
          but this twig
draws my attention,
really impresses me.
Older stuff
would have cracked,
but not this green: it knows how
to breathe in deep
crystalline air

and make no bones
about it.

It knows it's high time
       to start growing again
            toward higher stature,
       to get saturated
in this optical osmosis,
which some call breath
and others air.

But I say where
is there not
       change
and from what source
does all this spring?
This twig
that breaks out
without even breaking
but with just enough force
to kick the snow aside
and keep me still,
              makes me wonder.

I endow it
with joy,
unweighted delight,
so it is endeared
to me.
There's a story
behind every bump in nature:
           sudden jumps
      have their reason.

The sun did nothing unusual,
just continued to bleed
this winter cloak away
till new life
sprung seed
from water:
 a twig that throws corn snow!

First Snow in Two Years

Le lendemain: the day after tomorrow

Anticipation
is a long slow cloud churn
teaching French phrases:

the *future proche*—
il va neiger.

Blanket the horse
with a green muddy winter-weight
blanket (the name of a town in Texas).

When snow melts in Kansas
there's mud but no complaint,
just enough water
for a stay of execution,
saving the winter wheat.

Near me in the District
it's only rain,
and all the yards in Rockville
are now just slush.

Neanmoins it was enough
to spring out children,
ephemeral as flowers—
a sled ride, a wet dog,
a carrot nose.

So circle them round
their snowman,
take a pic and share it,
mark it *cherish.*

School will open sooner
than the day after tomorrow,
which no longer is
le lendemain.

Nones: **Morning song**

(*Nones: Roman 5th or 7th of the month*)

Somewhere
in the morning swirl,
leaving home,
a sluggish squirrel
near wheels and whirl—

scrunched away!
and Saturday with all its hopes
unfurled:
none other than this
morning song,
morning song!

Somewhere
beneath
a veil lifted
from gray business
and saved me
from the humdrum,
the neck aches,
the ashes of yesterdays'
hearth fire.

A song unexpected,
a brief reminder that no more
"your time will come"
or "time will tell"
could cure me

of this morning song,
this self,
moving
from the yawning hiatus,

whether it be Nones
or unknowns.

De Amicitia

for Audrey

Picking
snarly snaps
in a drought,
hair bleached out,
you're still honoring
your commitments:
a wedding tomorrow,
footprints in sand,
a honeymoon that memory never erased,
and an extra pair that appeared like an angel,
kept going.

Like this one more row
of snapdragons,
seemingly endless,
dusty yet so alive,
thirsty and not knowing
where the line break is,
or just where
one row begins
and another ends,

because with you, A.
it's just not that way,
and maybe that is why

you keep them
going.

Clear

(flying north from Israel, 1978)

From this far away
it looks clear and simple,
a patchwork quilt
of cultivation:
fields harrowed
fields lying fallow
fields touching fields,
small differences.

Reading the mountain's ridges
is like interpreting photographic maps'
peculiar contours,
no space between the lines.

How easy from here, this high,
to forget the fluid markets,
sandal slap on stone,
the curb man's music.

How easy it is,
above the sirens' reach,
above the wail in human speech,
how easy it is
to forget
firstborn, the flute,
the waters' music.

Time changes as we chase the sun.
Even mountains' shadows shrink
leaving us more time

to think: infinitely mythical
we become less real,
more horrific.

We think ahead
to where we will be
so that
if and when
suspended animation stops
we might be
tucking our would be children in bed
somewhere far off and secure
from the humdrum life of a hot dry land,
so that
if and when
someone shows us photographs
of our dreams—
illusive light that shines under our fingers
and is borne away
like sand by wind—
our hands that hold
the morning paper
might not shake
nor grasp the reality
this world has to offer.

We say we are just
moved to tears
reading the ruin, that is,
fresh stuff like this
morning's news: a nightmare
of destruction.
We have let gravity pull

bombs to fertile fields
and people, dismembered
unfamiliar faces, are blown away
like angels,
poor devils.

From this far away it looks so clear.
And I can count the mountains' backs…like camels.

First frost

for Pindie

First frost
on the barbeque cover:
a milky way galaxy
on whose edge we live.
It's almost dawn,
the motion detector
lights come on,
the puppy pees—
water calls water—
say the Japanese.
Morning dishes stacked,
I turn on the dishwasher,
get ready to vote—it's Election Day,
whom shall I choose?

I choose you:
two mounds of Venus,
invoking Monte Testaccio in Rome,
mountain high piles
of pottery shards—not ostraka
cast for exiles.

We two crones wear purple,
sipping warmed wine
by a steamy Swiss lake
where dawn still wears neutral colors,
and our lives are opaque
as the three far-flown daughters
who live outside us now,
at the edge of this our first frost.

Remember to forget: choosing *Lethe*

Remember to forget:
lithe bodies
nimble minds,
the sticky notes
that bind us
beyond our control.
Dad's ubiquitous
Don't Forget notes
all over the house,
our sole phone's
black curly cord
shining with voices
untangled if pulled
under the hall
bathroom door
where on the throne
we daughters adapted
conversational tones
to the faucet murmur,
beyond his earshot
yet still
umbilical.

Entrenched behind
his rough cut pine board,
he invented the first laptop.
Brow raised, head down,
his *Oh-my-aching-back*
supported by curvature
of a uniquely dehisced
rust-orange Citroën chair,

Dad often read for hours,
underlined in red,
then would date, clip, tape and place
the consumed victims
into wire baskets
until, troughs spilling over,
clippings systemically disappeared
into bulging green vertical files
near his big desk
in our living room.

Dad faced the sidewalk,
curtains open, sentinel.
Oversize art books
layered in a niche to his left,
Encyclopedia Britannica
tightly vertical on his right,
soldiers at attention,
next to the vestibule,
the front hall closet.
Now Dad sits
with his back
to the window
in a wing chair
in someone else's house,
holds a sky blue
plastic velvet lap desk
where he reads big print books,
turning page after page,
marks time with a well-placed
laminated bookmark,
its pressed flowers chosen
by a watchful woman, his wife

of sixty-some years.
You ask what can he remember?
Last autumn when I asked him
what are you thinking of?
Dad looked with a smile,
uttered two words
Buddha-style :

Perfect Love.

Sirmio
   (after *Catullus 31* – near his *Lares*/ home on *Lago di Garda*)

Heaven knows
we each seek a soul mate
in the unclaimed
hour.
Every tight lipped
thin lined stream of particle
star light bounds
light years past
to orb,
          cycle,
                    spire,
expire,
thrown as petals,
light prisms
intersecting our lost earth:
shining here and now,
then and there
to our eyes,
undying.

The same light still streams
past Catullus' favorite point—
Sirmio—near where we now gather,
hoping not to find it some day
smothered in Milan's outskirts.

Starlight here reaches true North,
a shepherd finds crown jewels,
though returning home penniless,

happy with his lyre,
old friends held fast.

After so long held apart in distant provinces
small godsends are heartening:
scent of spring,
fresh longing,
a quiet, rediscovered cove.

Six Wallflower Poems
(composed for Michelle Montalbano's, art show - lithographs)

1. First Impressions

The dress is
headless,
no body,
yet
feet still
floating
in memory
of dances
torn
from a page.

2. *Wallflower*

Wallflower
is a compound word.
There are so many:
Invisible fence
marked fragile,
instinctively clinging
to a wall,
blooming
just this once,
quietly, timeless,
fragile and fragrant
as a midnight rose,
alone
despite all the rehearsals.

3. *Dance of the Vein Dress*

Where's my body?
My buddy? Somebody?
Without partner
I am memory
translucent,
tangential,
irrelevant.

The dance is over,
yet still I hang,
singing like a music box
when someone opens
the closet:

"Don't tread on me.
You are walking all over me.
My folds drip
blind crevasses of blood
for you who let me
fall
when we dipped."

What happened?
Why am I here?
Tendrils on a hanger,
left hanging.
I'm not
Ripstop,
you know.

4. *Earth tones*

Rivulets, taffeta, *tango* (means "I touch"),
I want dance, earth tones of Latin:
Salsa, mambo, merengue,
But here I am, headless, cold shouldered,
cleft and left
like a spring flower mown down
by the careless plow
at meadow's edge.

5. *Roots after all (Resolution)*

My Heroine, it's okay
to be a wallflower!

You are not a compound word,
this is not a jail or a closet or a wall
you are up against!

You are experiential,
experimental,
luminous, transcendent!
You are the forget-me-not dress
ever mindful of your roots,
and there you stay
through all the different
shades of the seasons,
growing strong,
growing wall wise.

6. *Im Winter, Going West*

Im Winter hour, I crave sun.
Leaving dawn to Washington's gray
rain-drenched snow, I fly west,
gain a few hours,
to learn that your lithograph,
the yellow one,
has yet another variant.
In my wanderlust
I stumble upon it.

Erysimum asperum (harsh)
Eyrsimum nivalis (snowy)

are the Irish twins
of the mustard family,
each with a raceme
of yellow crucifer flowers,
each with its own
home—

the one, a sagebrush, subalpine,
the other, alpine meadows.

Both bloom in sundrenched spring,
lemon yellow
with pod-like fruit,
each on a pedicel,
like the mustard seed—
a whorl, a world of its own.

And then there's me!

Strung by Invisible Vision

(Martha's Vineyard – a pen and ink)

This place of clay cliffs,
lava colored collapse,
sags toward the surf.

Walking beach-wise
a bare ribbed woman
stalks to dig a face—

the clay:

an old man's locks,
dribbling, steel gray,
soft after rain,
erode into rivulets of a frown,
erasing his stare,
staying her eyes.

Her own face wilts away,
sinking to a watercolor world:

her inscape of silence
escapes compression,
and her turquoise eyes,
strange beads,
are strung
by invisible vision.

Spirit

(at Tanta Alice's cabin)

Birches of Bennington
feel so far away.
Here it's all black plum and locusts
gnarled by constant gusts from Gay Head.
Lovely to share this life with friends,
hearthfire to fight the frost.
We spin pointless stories, etch images
that emerge from memory.
Admire, wordless, a communion.
You pass among us, a smile
playing on our lips.

Clean

I wash myself under
waterfall of sound:
thrush, wind, wood,
dreams swim away.
Clock resonance matches
the tick of thicket birds
while my new day's gait
brushes grass.

Young Woman Jogger

I know also
total abandonment,
both sides:

the sudden freedom
that comes in a glimpse
of the world's spaces—

your own breath
on a cool morning
as you run beneath
an avenue of trees,

or that moment when

somewhere in between

the beginning
and
the going on

we stop,
        falter,

find.

Orange from Rome

(Lemington Spa)

On the edge of the bed I sat,
tiger skin wastebasket between my knees,
to catch the orange peels as they fell.

The orange from Rome.

I had locked the door
and opened carefully,
afraid to be disappointed.

Bright skin,
soft touch,
not too thick,
not too thin,
the skin fell
in three pieces.

And I hold you.
I smelled you,
twirled my tongue round
every section,
and suddenly I was rocking
slowly softly silently
on the edge of my bed
with the pleasure of a small
child,
I, unconscious,
felt that orange,
felt you,
felt freedom,

felt to feel,
felt.

God, it is good to feel again.

Thank you, blistering Roman sun
who numbs the mind,
tans the hide
and creates the orange
which came to me today
filling me with passion
and thought and love,
so far away,
where another orange sun is climbing...
climbing,
        climbing
in hues of yellow, white,
                        nothing,
and will return orange

there,
        then halve
                then slip
                        each section -
ever so quickly it sinks
into his ocean.

"Sea!" the English say, "Sea!"
but it's Ocean to me.

I know how far it is.

But, oh Lord, thank you for these ramblings.

This morning when I began to walk away
a voice from the pavement said,

"Cool my wrists and wash my feet,"

and I knew that everything would be
alright.

Two Gorges

1.
Ithaca is gorges.

The ubiquitous
bumper sticker
won't let me
forget my roots,
hometown shale and shallows,
a catalogue of creeks,
old swimming holes:
Six Mile, Flat Rocks,
Cascadilla, Taughannock,
Buttermilk, The Enfields.
What have I forgotten?
My hometown still holds places
where no one ever goes:
nameless tracks turned deer trails,
the same places
where "just last week"
we scrambled through,
thirty years later,
pushing on
our teenage children,
trying to find one emerald pool:
Potter's Falls,
where, through tunnel and light,
we as teens once dove,
swam against the funneled
dark current,
stroking down, through and up
to reach the light green light

surface, the other side,
always to emerge
breathless,
under its waterfall.
Today somehow
our trail went wrong,
and that shifty swimming hole
with its long history of
treacherous ledges,
remained elsewhere,
still, mythical, eluding both
of our memories, both
trial and error.

2.
Tabula Rasa (Clean Slate)

Of course, there's more
to my hometown than this.
it is a very vertical place
but one where people still can
gouge out a living
before dying *between* the gorges.
There's a think tank or two,
Llenroc and *I See*
where people work slate or ivy,
making books or reading them,
whirling atoms
or oh just listening
to the wind
in lake reeds.

Therefore, make no mistake,
Ithaca is more than mirroring *gorges*:
it's snow and ice,
Latin and Greek,
green apples and white grapes,
chestnut horses, wild flowers. . .

but all these things,
like memory,
form a slippery slope
and another poem,
or two, or three,
might just be
still waiting,
wading,
inside me.

Setting the Clock Ahead
(after Horace *Epistle II.1* – A walk in the Forum)

Spring forward,
fall back,
keep looking
for a soul mate.

Spring forward a poem
for the hour
lost or gained
but beware: memory is
a powerful sloth
hanging nose down
from a semiotic clothesline.

(Exempla gratia)...
Walking down a street
you notice a certain something
and the next thing you know
swift as thought
Nous has taken you
to a far away place
in the back of your mind
as if clicked on a link
that's active:

the midnight rose
unbroken ivory
poised above a crumbling
red brick Georgetown walk
transports you to Israel
where he showed you how

it opens
    just
        this
           once
then spirals,
petals fall,
and before dawn
it's gone.

Setting the clock ahead,
stepping out alone
in the cold backyard,
all white snow and black night,
for some reason you pause

between trash and recycling
to search the sky
for a shy patch of stars —
the Sister Pleiades —
all seven nearly drowned
by a bicuspid moon,
yet you stand still
until you find them
dancing!

Suddenly you are gone again,
long hammertoe gripping
deep into the grass of wet familiarity,
balancing on a dewy summer lawn
as you cross a shared crunchy driveway
to where once we stood
craning our necks —

me, a new initiate
in the art of focused patience,
you, my sole sister,
big sister of the long black hair,
Bettina, firstborn,
serendipitous and unlikely
prodigy of wise Athena—

we are together again,
side by side,
star grazing.

Physics Farmer

Pre-depression
he didn't know nothin'
about tractors.
When the economy flipped
he rolled over one morning
sayin': "Dear wife,
we need chickens to survive—
this slaughterin' business
sounds profitable and anyhow
I've lost my job.
Yesterday."

So they left the St. Lawrence greens,
the sea way
for other fields,
where they found Ellis,
another hollow: full green
and root ridden as any Amazon.
He planted weeds
of deadly night shade family
and hacked away
a road: together
they found a tomato patch,
and a hatchery,
a hatchery so full of chicks…

the poor woman nearly went blind
looking for babies, spent
hours in the basement
candling eggs
till the whites of her eyes

were just as red
as the capillaries in calcium shell,
if she found any,
and the man, his hands
like old knots
were never untied,
always busy, alone in the rustle
of corn.

Alterations on a Wedding Dress:
Qui Futurus Es Iam Fis

It's a tall order,
fitting the bill,
daughter *Oeconomica*
of hand-me-down-clothes.
Today it's time
for alterations,
making a wedding dress fit,
though clothes don't make
the woman.
My dreams haunt me,
icons of compromise:
corned beef cans,
a bucket of margarita mix
pulling me down to earthly life,
while this white dress has become
a beacon of wishes:
dreams come true!
Knowing that somehow
between your pragmatic realism
and my longing for mutual music,
(whole notes, solitude, breathing
in and out)
this wedding day will bring us
limping out of night.
And the fleeting freedom
to be who we really are
will sink in: you already are
just that: when
the life partner
you have chosen

chooses you –
there is no other choice!
The realm of dreams
kicking you at night
is just real enough
to knock you out of bed
and makes sure you write
this down:
qui futurus es iam fis.

(Who you will be you are already becoming.)

Replenish

a birthday poem for Geoff

May to mid-September
Maryland's sunshine
came north with you.
When will it end?

The drought, that is.

With winter snows?

For now we nestle
near our pasture of thistles,
boundless goldenrod.

Two horses paired up
under an almost-full moon,
eating, eternally green.

Hope springs: celebrate!
A new ring of grass circles
the dry crater pond.

Go now and wear out
those new Edgewater boots,
imagine cat-tails and grass carp
pulling down the undulating stars.

Well water, ring, sauna,
soapstone wood stove, all these acts
merit a moment, soon to call out:
champagne on the porch!

Our love can rest just long enough
to replenish.

August Freedom Dream

Augusts cross section neatly,
like growth on a lumbered tree:
the memory stump betrays summers' increase.

This is a lean summer for the South.
Its drought shall be remembered in more
than these annals of fingernail width.

Yet to me in the watery tropics
of our nation's capitol,
drought is an absence beyond imagining.

It is as unimaginable
as an empty church on Sunday,
as fuzzy as an unclean lens.

This morning, guilt-tinged but irrefutable,
a tear sprung from my left eye
as the moon shaped sacrament

melted on my palate,
for I knew its color
was that of wet sand:

my thoughts were with
the shimmer of northern beaches,
Menemsha, Gay Head, and images of freedom.

She Walked Alone to the Wharf
for Sarah

She walked alone to the wharf
   to watch the setting sun
and stayed long after to seize
   the foaming figurations
   water pouring over rock
   and the dappled sea

      turned
   a perfect star

Grazeland

The place you call Grazeland
holds seven horses now,
fattening before winter's onslaught.
The fence line backs up to the land
where we rode together
on one horse,
yours,
bareback.
Now I weave through
fifteen hand high thorns,
a nightmare to land in,
keeping arm's length away
when I can.
You redirect me to ride other ways,
to find trails and re-cut some
you almost mowed.
Two women friends I have to ride with now,
and more white horses.
You say another gray mare's arriving soon,
and I'm beginning to make some sense
of your absence, beginning even
to believe
it's irrational to feel
that wanting three or four words
 [(I love you (too))]
was ever important,
as I keep trying
to stay
on the same page
with you.

Afterword: Costa Rica

In the stillness
between thunderclaps
I remember
the *caballeros*—

a flitting swallow
redoubles
its course.

Activity can only
camouflage truth.

It's *sound* that
truly challenges:
a cowbell,
the bass of a car
stereo,

find me,
take me back.

The Castle near Bergamo

Flying east in June,
losing six hours
give or take a minute,
I reflect on the lake
near Bergamo, walled hill town,
the point of my conception.

Walls of flaming orange
camellias
reframe the small black and white
portrait of my mother,
her profile uplifted in light
dreamier than *Casa Blanca,*
a cameo
on a wet spring day
at *Villa Carlotta.*
She is our Lady of the Lake,
offsetting perennial melancholy
with walks in a high walled labyrinth
of azaleas
grown intertwined
toward light unquenched by the storm.

We three stood there
waiting as if for a concert to begin.
Me, newly a teen, in red raincoat
with buttons of brass.
Mom, wet face with remnants of a wintry tan,
hair blown out in tinted rainbows.
Dad, tight chested in all-weather coat,
sharing the big black umbrella.

Wind gusts spike
as we wait it out
to capture her
painstakingly
in the dark *camera*
hanging from his neck.

A Hurricane Came

(after *Horace Ode I.5*)

A hurricane came
from inside me last night:
I was the eye of the storm
until, passing through me,
all parts soaked and shuddered,
even my shuttered windows unlatched.
A tsunamis, a harbor wave,
left me high and dry on wet sand,
unharmed, just amazed
at how I got there.

Later, with armfuls of sheets,
I hung my towel out,
remembering vaguely
a poem Horace once wrote
about a sailor tying up his wet clothes
at the temple
in devotion
for having survived
a shipwrecked love.

The flood subsided,
leaving me
treasuring the line
yet bashful at my own
high water mark.

Wind Never Forgets

for Geoff

Wind never forgets its path,
old red barns blister
both winter and summer.

Your favorite subject—
was it recess?—
outside chasing around
balls and butterflies.

Now with pinball flappers
you lean in
to make the game last longer
and the lights shoot out,

and like two comets,
you and I change constantly,
straying just enough
to keep this
our love on course.

Crescent Trail Poem

Running down the Crescent Trail
much warmer than I'd thought,
just before Dalecarlia tunnel
wind zipped off my cap,
my hand caught
a spinning pinnate
brazen yellow.
Images fused like bone
clapped together over and over,
the slap of vertebrae shrinking,
expanding—a runner's dreamscape.
Why do we run?
We are captured in a dream:
Today's trail riddled with leaves,
our fortunes unstrained
in a bottomless cup of tea.

On the way back I stop cold:
a new bench, its bright plaque

In memoriam Jane Sisco 2008
   Long may you run

boldly etched, tells me everything,
explains the unanswered calls.
The last time I saw you was at our gym,
you were bruised wholly green,
told not to run any more,
going in for a brain scan.
That was the last time we spoke
until now—this brazen new bench invoking

a shock of tears, silent, insistent:
rest and go on. Why do we run?
To keep balance in our lives, seek peace
in jagged constellations underfoot.

Jane, *I saw the most beautiful things on the trail today.*
Shall I tell you?
Two deer eating among the kudzu undetected,
and the runners I saw today,
even before your bench found me
this warm November afternoon,
seemed unusually friendly.

Exhalations on a Power Line

I.

My first day off school I drop my daughter at Jet Blue,
saddle up the horse, head towards the Giant by way of the
woods.
Bright dew shines in long grass up the power line,
a solo purple morning glory thrusts out from blackberries'
edge,
concave silvery nets scattered like mini trampolines
wedge between damp weeds and stray buckling wheat.
Today I turn away to take it all in, go past to explore
the spotless grounds of the nearby Primitive Baptist Church:
daintily we skirt their fresh Meeting House,
slow between two wells, slip past the green graveyard,
until I glimpse a small headstone whose words are barely
worn:
a couple died two years apart (1876 - 1924/1926)
not so uncommon: his story became hers, lost and found.

II.

I think of my granddad outliving two wives,
parachuting with the Red Cross at fifty-five
how he alone swam the Sauer
under machinegun fire,
twice out, twice back,
in long johns, on his waist a rope
to tie around the far shore's tree,
line for a bridge,
saving untold lives.

No official soldier,
but on the down low
President Truman slipped him
a Bronze Star.

III.

Emboldened, we head back
to the power line
for a little lope,
then a fiery hand-gallop
up soft, dark, earthen trails,
slowing to dainty across pot shards
and broken glass
leached out from old soil
by fresh-cut ruts,
jarred open
from the recent plague –
dirt bikes.
Our simple horse trail
has been taken over,
multiplied into looped knots.
The screaming ATV's
create faux creek beds,
crack dried mud pools,
scatter rock, strip roots from earth
made smooth and slippery
as a wet gym floor.
Toward the top of our loop,
slowing from canter to trot -
there's an unmistakable sound: "Bees!"
big-bodied wasps streamline, keep our pace,

three or four, …don't count, don't look back!
Move out! into extended trot,
knock through even these roots
so fast we can lose them.
And we do come through
as from a dream,
whistling soft as prayer.
The morning's quiet now holds the usual sounds:
cars whir, trucks grind. But our mare, Sister Leto,
in her familiar language
snorts three times, walks loosely, well knows
that now
we're headed home.

First Anniversary

for Geoff

Golden or not, this is our first!
Better than silver or pearls
is the image of you
fishing today
next to me
on the same river
on currents that
eddy and stream
over each other
over and under
making love
seem so
easy:
it just goes
on and on
with no
particular
end.

Best laid plans
are laid aside
it's almost July
yet the fields lie
wet with fresh hay.

Tonight's early
fire works
usher in the holiday,
an early display
of confidence: it's summer,

things will go well,
we are
here to spell
a story not to listen
to one.

So may our love
in cosmic currents
keep bringing us
along
this same great river.

Hope is in the Healing

Hope is in the healing,

the looking up
when the horse trips
going over the triple spread.

Remember what the Good Book says:

keep your chin up
and be grateful
for the forgiving ground,
the dark tumble of earth
that absorbs
the curl of our spines
as we roll
earthbound
in an indoor ring
where the ground
is not frozen
this winter,
and like memory,
keeps coming back
to me.

Looking into the Banks of Your Eyes
                        (after reading Plato's *Ion*)

Looking into the banks of your eyes
a River runs between us
as we stand still.
There is no time.

I can trace love in your hair.
It is red, it is real.
The cobwebs snap softly, noiselessly.
Where two falls intersect,
higher and lower, harmony.

Religion is spiritual capitalism, you say.
For what we've found, stumbled into,
there's no other word but Grace.
I've kept myself alive for this.
(And to think I even thought
I could write poetry alone.)
Anima mundi. Bare skinned baby.
Ankles initiate into the creek.
It's all interwoven
and we don't know
how deep it is yet *(heti).*

Melchizadek

for my students at B-CC and Newfield (D. C., 1987)

Melchizadek, a man in your line walked past the picket.
Now avenues carry his name, ringing like a liberty bell:

Dr.- Martin - Luther – King, - Jr.

In Cumming, Georgia, this January,
a ripple returned
to raise the dead-best-left-forgotten
hero: your spirit!
Marching like kudzu,
overtaking fields of indifference,
they strode up the white highway of supremacy,
till, fluttering from the highest tree, they spoke out—
on things as they were and are and soon would be.
From Washington, on TV
I saw their streamers,
saw cause to celebrate
the anniversary of his birth,
but outside the Capitol
the streets were quiet
as if this day was cursed.

My small class of schoolchildren
still protected from despair
were assigned to piece together
who was this MLK, they
asked my age when he was shot
and why did people shatter
the windows on the streets
knocking out their own teeth?

And today I swore I heard his voice,
gutsy, deep, still angry,
kicking up the litter and autumnal leaves,
(Jesus turning the moneylenders' tables,
cleaning house)
in a gust of wind in Farragut Square.

Moon Blind Mare

for Debbie

Diagnos*is* is a Greek word
(as *is* anything that ends in *"-is"*).

A best friend for twelve years
turned twice that
but within the span of two raggedy autumns
she—Leopard Appaloosa that she *is*—
had recurring *uvitis.*
Her eye twice daily anointed,
with triple antibiotics
named of ancient Greek roots:
*Opt*imune, Flurbi*profen*, Atro*pine*.

She grazes unflinchingly,
keeps her head down, all business.
Hungry as a bear, that mare!
Had she been one of Diomedes'
flesh eating fillies
we'd all be dead!

Sister Leto *is* a bit indifferent
to my call in all seasons
except winter, but comes into season
every moon.
Near the geldings' pasture gate,
she nickers, flirts, stands and squirts.
But her best friend forever is another app
about half her age. They go way back.

In winter her white coat brightens,
blends with the snow when she runs
into the wind faster than spit can freeze.

Prognosis for Moon Blindness?
Many remedies but no cure… the mystery *is*
there *is* no cure though known
as the oldest documented disease
among domesticated animals:
ancient Egyptians recorded their dismay
at the sudden loss of sight in healthy horses,
inexplicable and random
as the plague-bearing arrows
borne by far-shooting Apollo.

We now know Moon blindness
occurs most often in Paints and Apps.
But the Irish believe a white horse *is*
magical.

Our *Sister*, she is just that,
though it's all we can do
to keep her right eye alive.

For the left eye is
too late to bring back:
faded blue globe, icy pale,
color of old denim,
still blinking.

At night under twinkling stars
I come out to the barn late
to see how she's doing.

I find her easily,
immortal green but gentle,
warm my hands
in her barrel chest,
then cross under her neck
and sing

"My Bonnie lies over the ocean…"

tired and sometimes teary
but happy to be there,
knowing she knows
just where *I am.*

Hawk's Vision: *im Winter*

She has the imagination
of a bird in flight
but the heart of a quail.
Words come to her
like snowflakes
skewered on her eyelashes,
soon melting.

This morning
while she walked to the brick house
what she thought was
a large Gray Hawk
circled far above the school flag,
red, white and blue.
Suddenly the dawn sun opened one eyelid,
spilling Sicilian oranges
through moon-soaked woods.

The hawk became a Red Tail,
molting on winds of welcome *Januarius*,
first rising, then dipping
above copper-edged chimneys,
circling the rippled stripes and stars
for what seemed to be forever,
eyes stripping bare the oak-strewn grass,
searching to divulge secrets.

Was it a shiny chariot that stirred his valence,
as he hovered above the central drop-off point
where teens clad in watch plaids kilts
poured from doors to a room called home?

Or was it simply a hawk's vision—*im Winter*—
preparing to dive and claw
an inadvertent mouse,
the simple *mus* diving beneath
a windblown candy wrapper.

Tell me, she whispered to the wind,
I have to know.

One Day You Wake Up: Upstate

(after Prof. McConkey's story of
how he chose a place to settle down)

One day you wake up
to what this place is really about.

You check out the scene,
then, having scouted around,
you realize you'll have to leave.

Unless you marry into the small town myth
of agrarian endings.
Unless that ox-head falls off your engine hood
and you realize the anchor's in the soil
for good, and you start out

      with four good eyes.

Crazy Bird

The mimosa jay insists on testing illusion:
her own
reflection challenges from our picture window
that world
beyond her beck and call.

Porch Wood

On our long lost way
to cut the Christmas tree
the back roads splintered into shortcuts
only a mule could know.

Way back
from macadam roads the wooden shack
looked silvery in frozen sunlight,
yet its quartered wood stacked high
upon a seaboard porch
spoke preparation.

Winters never were like this,
everyone said, in Georgia,
but the board house knew,
it knew better,
whoever dared live there,
knew each chimney brick.

How long this house had howled,
nobody knew.
But a pig and a dog
on the lee side of the ditch
shared tangled cover in the naked berries
until the cold snap passed,
and porch wood
once again
sparked the hearth.

Sister's Dance

for Rachel

When the mind is
a closed door
another window opens:
your body
lets you in
lets you *step back,*
allow the doors to close.

When the mind can't
know because of numbness,
let your body lead:
sway gently
to this track,
white sounds
still hissing.

Minutes before
boarding this train
I was driving
against traffic
to meet you,
against a stream
of white lights.

I was (the only one) moving.

One hour before now
I was deep in woods
watching two grey herons
big as deer

fly overhead like dinosaurs
above me while
my sweet old mare, Sister,
a magic white horse,
kept dancing
under me
splashing in our stream.

A window, when it opens…

Stopping to Breathe

Stopping to breathe,
you envelop me
in your breath.

I am your watermark,
thin as paper,
shear as onion skin,
two-faced yet legible
as *Janus*
guarding the bridge.

Poems spring from silence
and little noises
that stretch time:
afternoon bird song,
the purr of a light plane
imagined beyond
white pleated blinds
make me think—
it must be a blue sky.

My daughter completed for me
the art of butterfly kisses
that I now pass on to you.
When, like trees,
we disentangle to grow
our separate ways,
remember these silences
timbered in peace
and desire.

Walton County, Georgia

Maybe the ribbon road
to *Good Hope* and beyond
really does turns through another world:
a forest of color gradations of green,
the road's graded pavement purring
under our old striped orange *Vega*
with its newly rebuilt transmission.

Merging into *Monroe* –
the watermelon stand,
people fixing a lace porch.
Everything's square
as a carpenter's angle,
freshly primed.
Hard Labor Creek State Park
is found in this New South,
like us, making our way
out of *Athens*
to where post civil war revitalization
still resounds with a hammer,
and love's labors
are not lost.

La Bocca della Verità

What you put in, you get out.
It's the same damn thing
with the bank.
The money machine,
like the *Bocca della Verità*,
may refuse my card
or swallow my hand
but it never lies.

Sometimes my right arm
feels like it's been cut off,
but its poison oak is all
that warms my bed.

Long conversations on the cell
make my ears burn
but only time is
and today's rice
in what once was
a shiny copper bottomed pot.
I try to throw it out
but like a babe in bathwater
it's still too precious.
So I leave the stinking house,
kitchen, rice pot, all to soak
in dusky sunshine.

Later, calmed by twilight, I realize:
money is not the answer,
only the refrain.
And so I pledge to refrain

from spending anything I don't have—
including you, the one I'm thinking of.

Minutes to Myself: when a "single" mother sleeps in...

Palinurus' song:

Praise the god of sleep and languor,
Praise the slow-heeled god of torpor.
Words that heal and words that bind
find me in the morning, kind.
Last night, feverish, I fell asleep;
today has found me breathing deep.
This white mound, and that, outside,
surround me! Quilts of air at will
sustain me! Make me your victim,
instrument, slave, and keep me
from a watery grave.

Sublime Chaucer:

After years of sleepless nights
my soul this day awakes,
and grateful, praises Sleep again
for being here, my friend.

White sails:

How good it is to have
these Minutes to Myself,
the whole house quiet
with sleeping children (three)
and my body eager only for this
languor: to stay in this white bed,

this pirate-fighting dream ship,
like the one that Robert Louis
Stevenson knew as a child,
celebrating imagination,
so too I am
celebrating, pushing off,
inaugurating a path
upon the deep.

Acknowledgments

The Avocet – A Journal of Nature Poetry (2017): "Hawk's Vision: *im Winter*"

The Avocet Weekly (2016-17): "*Nones*: Morning Song"; "Twig Poem"; "Young Woman Jogger"

The Journal of Modern Poetry (vol. 18, 2015): "Crescent Trail Poem"

The Journal of Modern Poetry (vol. 20, 2017): "First Frost"; "Sirmio"

New Writers (Ithaca High School literary magazine, 1974)*:* "She Walked Alone"

Rainy Day (Cornell University, 1977): "Physics Farmer"

Poems in my forthcoming chapbook *Choose Lethe: Remember to Forget* (Finishing Line Press, 2017): "Clean"; "*De Amicitia*"; "Exhalations on a Power Line"; "Hope is in the Healing"; "Moon Blind Mare"; "*Nones*: Morning Song"; "One Day You Wake Up: Upstate"; "Porch Wood";" "Remember to Forget"; "Twig Poem".

About the Author

Carolyn Clark was born in Ithaca, NY. She completed Classical studies at Cornell, Brown and Johns Hopkins (diss. *Tibullus Illustrated: Lares, Genius and Sacred Landscapes*, 1998). After raising children and teaching in Maryland, she now enjoys living with her husband Geoff in the Finger Lakes region.

CPSIA information can be obtained
at www.ICGtesting.com
Printed in the USA
FFHW02n0439230818
47947943-51632FF

9 781681 111957